Letter Aa Activi

Trace the letter

Find the letter

V	A	a
a	g	A
a	A	Z

Color the pictures

ax

ant

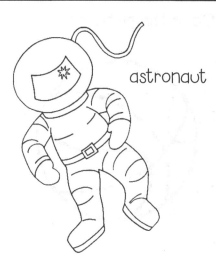

astronaut

alligator

apple

alphabet

Make a pattern

Letter Bb Activity Sheet

Trace the letter

Find the letter

B	b	p
b	D	B
u	B	b

Color the pictures

ball

bird

book

boat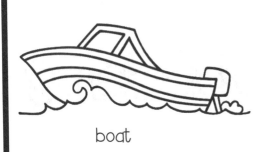

 bell

butterfly

Make a pattern

Letter Cc Activity Sheet

Trace the letter

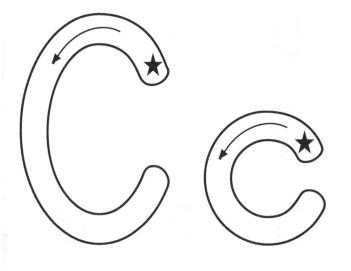

Find the letter

c   e   C

o   C   c

c   C   G

Color the pictures

cat

can

cart

corn

cab

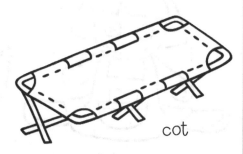

cot

Make a pattern

Letter Dd Activity Sheet

Trace the letter

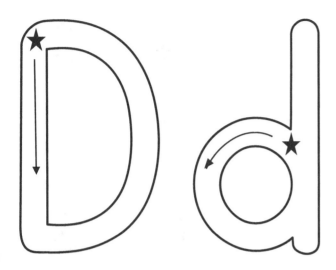

Find the letter

D	d	B
O	d	D
D	P	d

Color the pictures

dolphin

diamond

duck

doll

dinosaur

dog

Make a pattern

Letter Ee Activity Sheet

Trace the letter

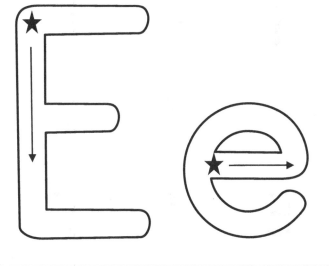

Find the letter

o	E	e
e	e	F
E	E	c

Color the pictures

elephant

exit

evergreens

elevator

egg

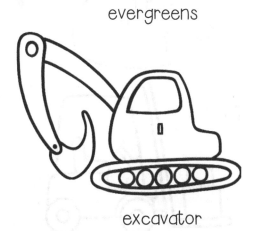
excavator

Make a pattern

Letter Ff Activity Sheet

Trace the letter

F f

Find the letter

t	f	F
F	T	f
E	f	F

Color the pictures

fox

 football

five

forklift

fire

fish

Make a pattern

Letter Gg Activity Sheet

Trace the letter

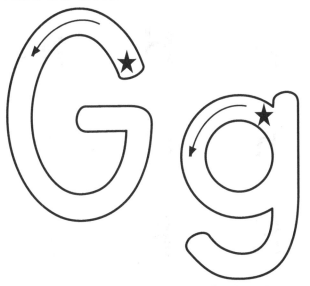

Find the letter

G	g	w
g	G	C
G	p	g

Color the pictures

gown

gorilla

game

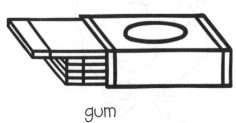
gum

goat

girl

Make a pattern

Letter Hh Activity Sheet

Trace the letter

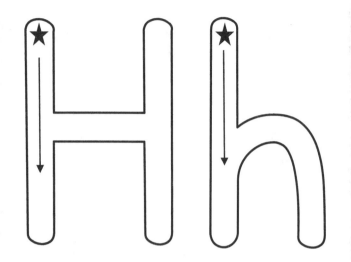

Find the letter

r	H	h
h	U	H
H	h	I

Color the pictures

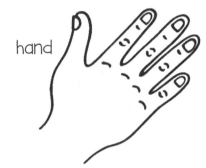
hand

heart

horse

house

hammer

hen

Make a pattern

Letter Ii Activity Sheet

Trace the letter

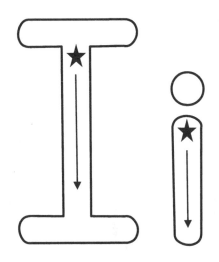

Find the letter

I	L	i
t	i	I
i	I	j

Color the pictures

interstate

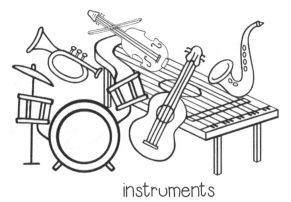
instruments

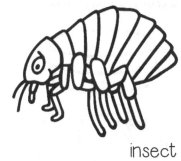
insect

itch

iguana

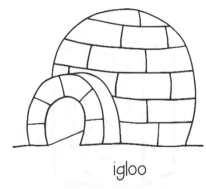
igloo

Make a pattern

Letter Jj Activity Sheet

Trace the letter

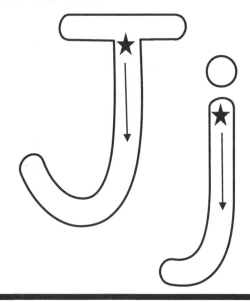

Find the letter

i	J	j
j	T	J
J	j	I

Color the pictures

jelly

jet

jog

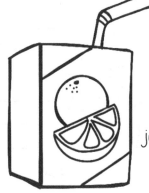
juice

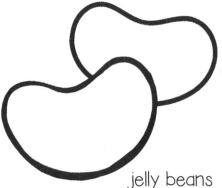
jelly beans

jug

Make a pattern

Letter Kk Activity Sheet

Trace the letter

Find the letter

K	h	k
N	k	k
K	w	K

Color the pictures

kite

keypad

kangaroo

kid

kitten

king

Make a pattern

Letter Ll Activity Sheet

Trace the letter

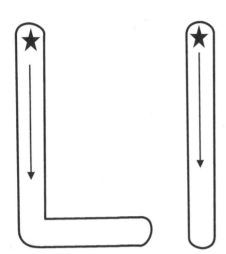

Find the letter

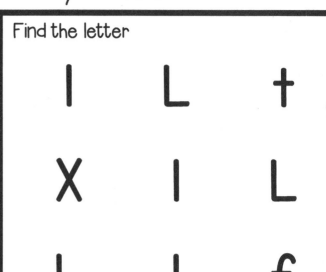

l	L	t
X	l	L
L	l	f

Color the pictures

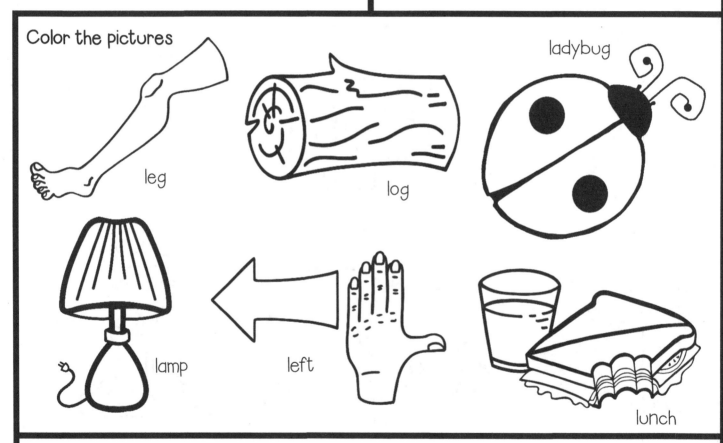

leg

log

ladybug

lamp

left

lunch

Make a pattern

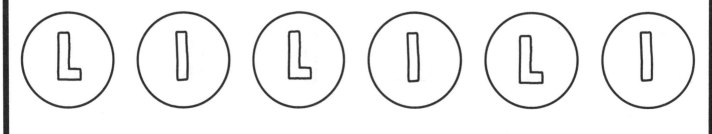

L l L l L l

Letter Mm Activity Sheet

Trace the letter

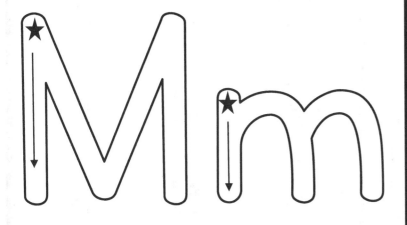

Find the letter

M	m	u
Z	N	m
M	m	M

Color the pictures

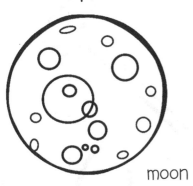

moon

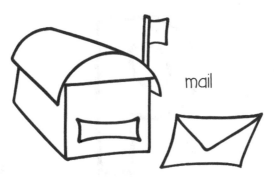

mail

mushroom

mouse

muffin

mop

Make a pattern

Letter Nn Activity Sheet

Trace the letter

Find the letter

M	n	N
Z	N	n
n	N	h

Color the pictures

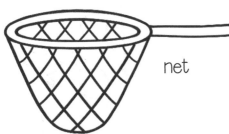
net

nine

nail
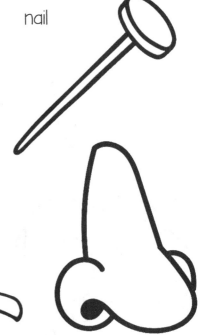

nurse

nest

nose

Make a pattern

Letter Oo Activity Sheet

Trace the letter

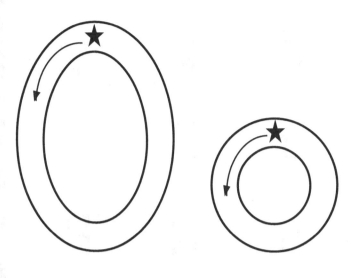

Find the letter

o	c	O
o	Q	o
O	O	g

Color the pictures

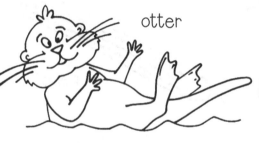
otter

olive

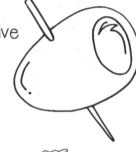

ox

octopus

ostrich

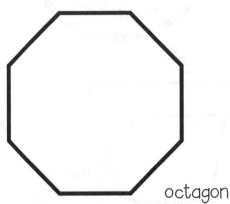
octagon

Make a pattern

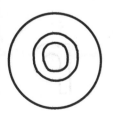 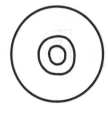  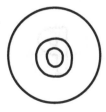  

Letter Pp Activity Sheet

Trace the letter

Find the letter

P	p	y
g	P	p
p	R	P

Color the pictures

pizza

pumpkin

pencil

pot

pig

popcorn

Make a pattern

Letter Qq Activity Sheet

Trace the letter

Find the letter

q Q q

Q j o

g q Q

Color the pictures

quiet

LIBERTY

quarter

queen

question

quail

quilt

Make a pattern

Q q Q q Q q

Letter Rr Activity Sheet

Trace the letter

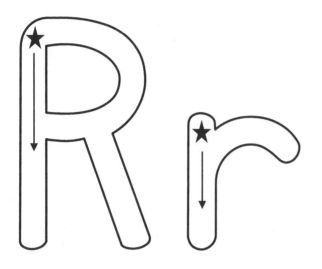

Find the letter

R	r	P
r	n	R
k	R	r

Color the pictures

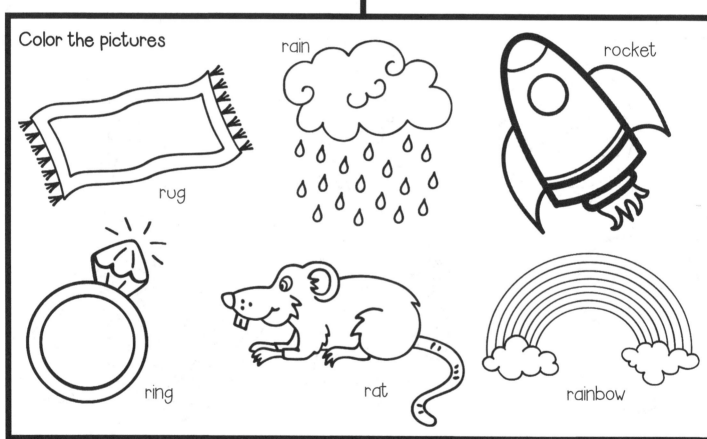

rain

rocket

rug

ring

rat

rainbow

Make a pattern

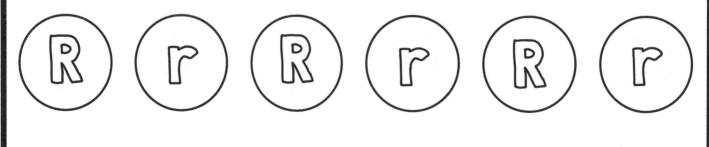

Letter Ss Activity Sheet

Trace the letter

Find the letter

s	S	z
C	S	s
S	U	s

Color the pictures

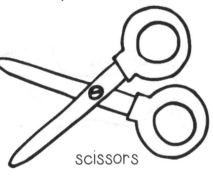

scissors

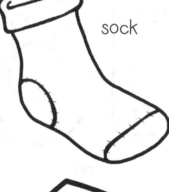

sock

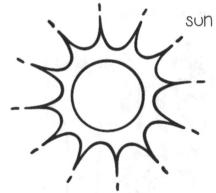

sun

soap

six

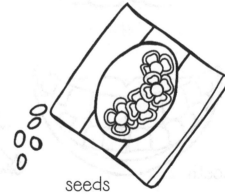

seeds

Make a pattern

Letter Tt Activity Sheet

Trace the letter

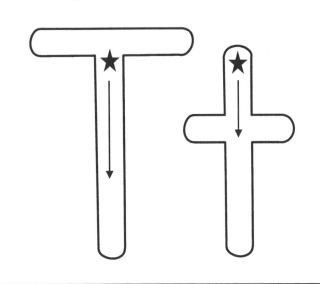

Find the letter

T	L	t
t	f	T
T	t	H

Color the pictures

tiger

ten

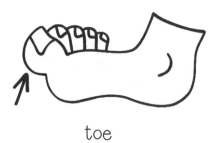

toe

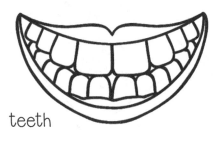

teeth

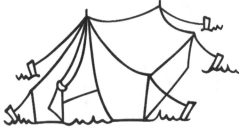

tent

turtle

Make a pattern

Letter Uu Activity Sheet

Trace the letter

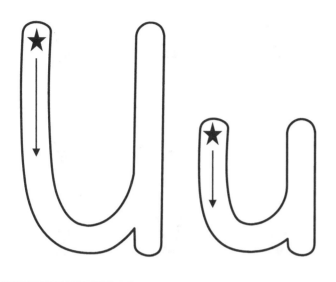

Find the letter

u	h	U
r	U	u
U	u	m

Color the pictures

under

umpire

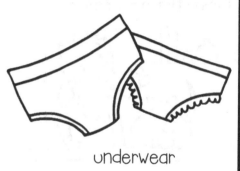
underwear

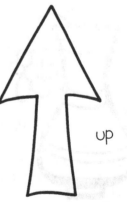
up

umbrella

abcde
underline

Make a pattern

Letter Vv Activity Sheet

Trace the letter

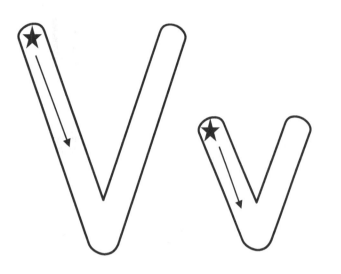

Find the letter

Y   v   V

V   x   v

v   V   t

Color the pictures

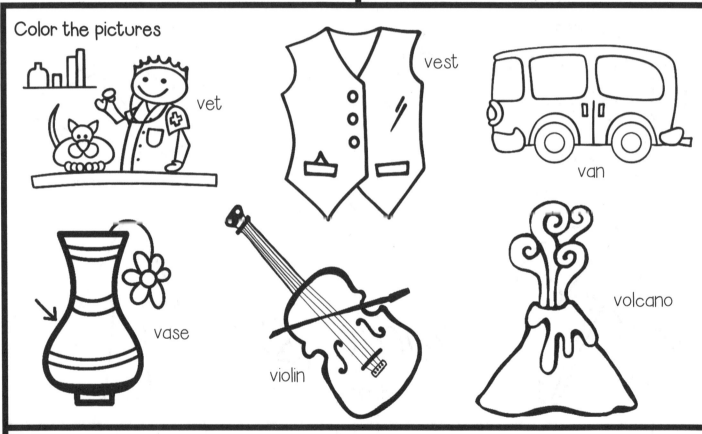

vet

vest

van

vase

violin

volcano

Make a pattern

Letter Ww Activity Sheet

Trace the letter

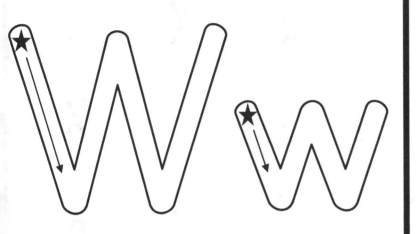

Color the pictures

wheel

wand

watch

wave

watermelon

wall

Make a pattern

Letter Xx Activity Sheet

Trace the letter

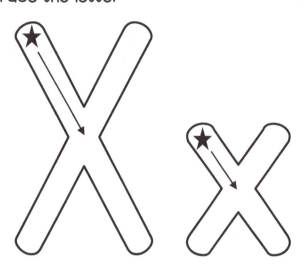

Find the letter

x	X	y
N	x	X
X	x	k

Color the pictures

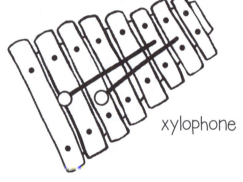

xylophone

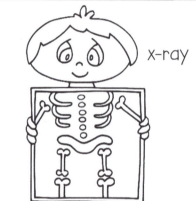

x-ray

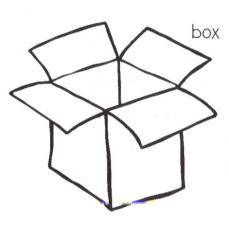

box

ox

fox

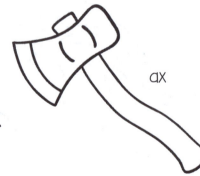

ax

Make a pattern

Letter Yy Activity Sheet

Trace the letter

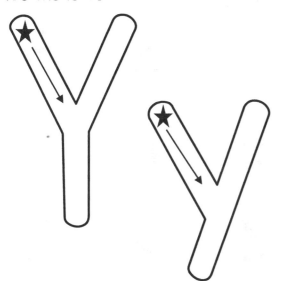

Find the letter

y	Y	g
y	T	Y
Y	y	v

Color the pictures

yak

yolk

yarn

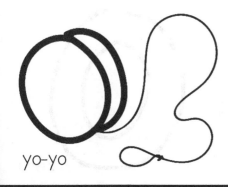
yo-yo

yogurt

yawn

Make a pattern

Letter Zz Activity Sheet

Trace the letter

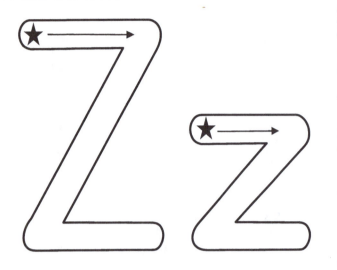

Find the letter

Z	z	F
z	k	N
Z	z	Z

Color the pictures

zucchini

zigzag

ZOO
zoo

zebra

zipper
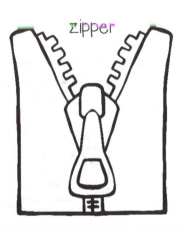

zero

Make a pattern